How to get more money than you can ever handle!

A real estate investor's guide to funding deals

By Ryan G. Wright

By Ryan G. Wright

COPYRIGHT

This publication is intended to provide accurate information with regard to the subject matter covered. It is offered with the understanding that neither the publisher nor the author is engaged in rendering legal, accounting or other professional services. If legal advice or other expert assistance is required the service of a competent person shall be retained.

This information provided for educational purposes only. Care should be taken by individuals to insure the concepts and principles taught herein do not conflict with new laws after the time of printing, or existing laws that may relate only to specific states.

While the author and publisher have taken precaution in preparing this information, the author and publisher assume no responsibility for errors or omissions, or for damages resulting from the use of the information contained herein.

By accepting this information you agree to indemnify and hold harmless the publisher, the author, accompanies the successors, assigns and affiliates, the forum and producers of all material which you obtained. You understand it is solely your responsibility to conduct yourself in a manner consistent with all applicable laws and that the presenters are not giving legal or tax advice. Should you misuse the information, fail to operate within the law, choose not to consult with an attorney, or suffer any damages whatsoever, you will be solely responsible.

Table of Contents

Section 1

You make money
when you buy...

Chapter 1
The Secret

It is not about finding the money; it's about finding the property.

So many real estate investors and potential investors today are missing the big secret. The secret is simple: It's not about finding the money; it's about finding the property.

Too many real estate investors are out there worrying about how they are going to fund the deal. Well, settle down. I can tell you, from 10 years of experience in the hard money lending business our phones and e-mail are flooded with hypothetical situations that may exist in the future. Very few inquiries are coming from people that actually have properties ready to finance.

I struggled to find financing during my early days as a real estate investor for the same reason. We would go to loan investors that could potentially fund deals for us, and waste time talking about imaginary scenarios that could potentially happen. We would talk about properties and what type of funding we would need. Some lenders were mildly interested, but all of them would ask if we had a deal on a property under written contract that they could look at. As you know, if it is not in writing, it is not under contract. If we were buying from a bank on an REO or short sale, they would want to see something in writing from the original bank saying they agreed to a discounted payoff. Well, I didn't have anything concrete; nothing in writing. I was caught in a Catch 22: I wanted to know if they would provide the funding so I could go out and find a deal, but they wanted a real deal to look at before they could let me know if they would fund it. It's simple business; they're not interested in my aspirations or "what if" scenarios; they are only interested in deals that are ready for funding.

So many real estate investors today are spending all their time, energy, and resources trying to find the money. They have it wrong! You have the secret right here in the first chapter of this book, and it is the most important lesson you need to learn to launch yourself on your way to successful and profitable investing. Bring a good deal to the table, and you will get the funding. The last thing you need to worry about is finding the money. Go out and find a good, exciting, deal. *Every good deal will get financed!*

Good deals mean profitable loans for hard money lenders. They are money magnets. Everything is attracted to them. Everyone is attracted to them. Money attracts money. Lenders can smell a good transaction, and your good deal, that has safety and protection for the lender, is exactly what they are looking for.

Spend your time, spend your resources, and spend your money finding good properties. If you find good properties, finding the money is simple. If you bring in a bag of gold dust, prospectors will invest in your goldmine. Money will be attracted to you and to your deal like a magnet. Simply put, funding will be found.

That's the big secret; plain and simple. It's not about finding the money; it's about finding the property. If you have a good deal, money will be attracted to the deal. Lenders are in the business of lending money—*that's what they want to do*. A good deal is easy—and I do mean *easy*—to finance.

Chapter 2

Find the deal and you will find the money

Imaginary situations are never going to make you real money.

There are so many real estate investors that are running hypothetical situations with this property or that property. The fact of the matter is that imaginary situations are never going to get you real money. You might have a great plan for investment properties in a certain county, neighborhood, or street, but no one is going to be interested in committing funding until you can plug a real property into the scheme and propose a real concrete deal. If you provide a lender with hypothetical analysis, the best he can give you is some talk about hypothetical money. If you really want to make money as a real estate investor, then go find properties, go find good deals, and put good deals under contract. Once you find good deals, finding the money is the simple part. We have seen brilliant investors who suffer from "analysis paralysis," working up complex spreadsheets before they would make an offer or even look at a property. Bring your ideas into the real world if you want to see real money.

I know it is frustrating when a lot of lenders out there will not make any commitment whatsoever. They won't even let you know what counties they will lend in, what states, or what prices. They won't be forthcoming with any information at all. All they will tell you is,"Hey, bring us the deal, and we will see." A lender should tell you what they are going to charge, what areas they are willing to service, and other parameters. Do you know what type of properties they will finance? Will they do commercial loans? Will they do multi-unit properties, or will they only do single family dwellings? What price range can a property fall into, and what charges do they add on? I think that is critically important information for you to know. If you are working with a good hard-money lender, you can get that information easily and make sure you are within their general guidelines. Good hard money lenders will post this right on their website for the world to see. This will make it unnecessary for you to waste time making phone calls and "interviewing lenders." You can get it all by the click of a mouse.

Again, we are not talking about analysis paralysis. We are talking about general, overall guidelines of what to look for. I can tell you from my own, personal, experience, I believe that you should be looking for single-family homes in major metropolitan areas under $250K. That's my belief, because I am convinced that when you find homes that meet those guidelines, you will be able to get funding on them very easily—as long as you purchase the property for the right price. So when it comes down to it, just find the deal and you will find the money.

Chapter 3
You have all the money you could ever need

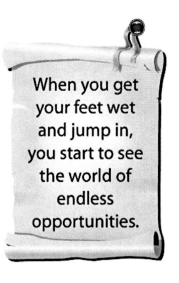

When you get your feet wet and jump in, you start to see the world of endless opportunities.

From my own experience as a real estate investor, I can tell you that, early on in my career, I was really concerned about having the money to close deals that took a lot of time for me to put together. I tortured myself about where and how I would come up with the money I needed to finance my hypothetical investment opportunities. Now, with more than a decade of experience investing in real estate, I know that that finding the money is the easy part; but the really great news I discovered is that there is so much money available it would blow you away. As hard money lenders we have people contacting our office that have several irons in the fire (potential investment opportunities), wondering if we have enough money to fund them. Our response is simple: Try and break the bank! No one has ever done it. We have not turned down a loan in over seven years because we didn't have money.

We funded every single deal, that met our criteria, every single time, no questions asked. Still, these hot shots keep calling and saying that they need so many loans, we'll never be able to fund them all. Our portfolio manager will tell you our pockets are deep, and they don't have holes in them. Once you get in the game, and get a good property under contract, money will find your deal, and you will be able to find more money than you can ever handle.

It's kind of like the ocean. If you have ever been on a scuba diving trip and looked out at the ocean from inside your boat, you've seen the water out there; it looks so beautiful, and you are looking for fish. You might see a dolphin. If you are really lucky, you will actually see a shark.

All you are going to see is that tip of the shark's dorsal fin poking out of the water. Beneath the surface of this vast ocean is opportunity that you can't even begin to see from the deck of the boat. Now, if you put on a snorkel mask and some fins and go out there snorkeling, you'll discover a whole new world you have never seen before. You are going to see schools of fish and coral. You are going to see all kinds of things that you didn't even realize existed when you were standing on the boat. It is only when you actually jump into the water that you are going to see this whole hidden world in the light of all of its possibilities.

If you get back on the boat, take off the snorkel and strap on some air tanks. As you start to scuba dive, you are going to go even deeper beneath the surface of the water than you can go with your snorkel. You are going to go pass all those small colorful fish. You are going to go under the coral, and you are going to see an octopus down on the bottom and a ship wreck. Here is where your treasure is going to be.

Real estate investing is kind of like our snorkeling or scuba diving. If you are standing in the boat and not engaged in the game, it looks like there is no opportunity out there to find funding. It may seem like you just occasionally see the dorsal fin of a shark. When you get your feet wet and jump in, you start to see the world of endless opportunities. As you get more deeply into it and start finding good deals, you will begin to see the whole world open up. The deeper you go, the more availability you will see. When it comes down to it, there is more money than you could ever handle. In real estate investing, all you need to fund your deals is a good property. Once you find a good property, you will find the money and there is more money than you could ever possibly dream of.

I can assure you from my own experience that there will be plenty of money if you find good deals. The hard part of being a real estate investor isn't finding the money to fund your deals. The hard part of being a real estate investor is finding good deals, and that is your job. As a real estate investor, you have one job and one job only: to find good deals, find good transactions, and find things you can make money on. If you can make money on it, then your lenders are going to make money on it, so your lenders are going to be willing to loan the money. Just like the ocean, there is more money out there than you could ever possibly handle for your real estate investment needs.

Chapter 4

Act like you have the money

Big Hat,
No Cattle

There is a common phrase that our Texas friends have taught us: "Big hat, no cattle." This phrase refers to those Texas cowboys that walk around with huge ten gallon hats on. It used to be the bigger the hat, the richer the cowboy. Well, now you see these guys with the great big hats walking around, but they have no wealth to back it up. It's all show. They have no ranch. They have no cattle. They have no assets. They have no money. But they sure look good, because they wear a big hat and they drive a big truck. I understand that everyone in Texas drives a big truck. Anyway, they've got the big hat, but no cattle. These guys would drive around in their big trucks, with their big hats, and act like they had the money, but you know what? If they acted the part well, they still got the attention, the girls, or whatever they might have been looking for. And that is exactly what you need to do as a real estate investor. Walk the walk and talk the talk of a successful, big time, real estate investor. Wear your confidence like a big hat, and exude the kind of competence that makes it seem like you have a big herd of cattle back at the ranch.

You need to make offers like you have the money. You need to look at properties like you have the money. You need to do everything you can to get good properties under contract— like you have the money. You need to wear a big hat, if that's what it takes to get good deals under contract. You can act like you have the money, because you do. When you find the good deal, you will find the good money. Money is attracted to good deals, so don't waste your time trying to figure out how to fund something that doesn't exist. Don't play around with hypothetical situations in an imaginary world and analyze a crazy situation that does not even exist.

Deal with things that are real—real, and under contract. Your job is to get that property under contract, and to do that you need to act like you have the money.

Just do it. Act like you have the cash. You need to act like you can go and close on these deals, because the truth is, *you can*. If you find a good deal, you will find the money; and there is more money out there than you could ever imagine for real estate investors with good deals. So wear a big hat, make the offers, act like you have the money, and you will be successful as a real estate investor.

Side Note: I am not suggesting or inferring that you need to go out and buy a big cowboy hat to wear around, and I am DEFINITELY not saying that you need to go buy a BIG truck to start as a real estate investor. Use what you have; don't go buy things that you might need someday.

Chapter 5
Proof of Funds

You have a
pretty big hat
there cowboy,
Lets see if you
got any cattle.

Now, as you drive around with your big cowboy hat on and you are talking about buying properties to banks or other lenders, there is going to come a time when a seller, whether it's a bank, an asset manager, or a private seller, is going to say, "You've got a pretty big hat there, cowboy. Let's see if you got any cattle. Take me back to the ranch; I want to see what you've got so I can make sure you have the cash to close on this deal."

When that situation happens, there's no need to panic. All you need to do is get a proof of funds letter. At DoHardMoney.com we have a proof of funds letter that you can download instantaneously. It probably takes about 10 or 15 seconds. You just put in the property address, your information, the amount of your purchase, and how much you think the property is worth. Then, simply certify that you understand the parameters—for instance, our loans are for single family non-owner occupied homes under $250,000, in certain areas of the country, all of which can be found on the website, and just click your acceptance and compliance with our guidelines. As soon as you click the button, it brings up a proof of funds letter. Your personalized proof of funds letter is typed up and signed in a PDF document from our portfolio manager. It states says that we have set aside the funds for your transaction, and once your transaction goes under contract, we will send our team out and provide funding within a short time frame. You can download as many of these as you want, as many times as you want, at any time of the day or night, and from any country anywhere. You could even be on vacation. Wherever you are, you can take off that big hat and show people your cattle, because if you have a good deal you can get the money to back it up.

What happens when you download that proof of funds letter? It actually logs into our computer system and records that you have proof of funds for that property. The seller can call our office and say, "I am calling you about Bob. He made an offer on my property, and he gave me this proof of funds letter. You know, he wears a really big hat; he gave us this paper that looks pretty legitimate, but I am just wondering; does he really have cattle?" We put the name into our computer system and pull up your proof of funds. We look at address and tell the seller that we have funds set aside for this transaction. Once it goes under contract, we only need to send our evaluators out there, and we can finalize. Does this proof of funds guarantee that you can get the financing? No. It says we have funds set aside ready to finance, as long as everything meets our criteria and as long as it is a good deal.

Again, the key to being a successful real estate investor is to focus on finding good deals. Find good deals, and the money will come. When the wheels of your deal start turning, we are able to verify that we've got funds set aside and that we are ready to go. We tell the seller calling to hurry and put the property under contract so we can get our evaluations complete and get the property closed and funded. We can show that you have the cattle sitting at home, and you can really perform on your proposal. Your offer will look pretty good in the seller's stack of offers with when you have proof of funds. You are going to have to talk to lot of people and work with lot of banks to get offers accepted, but, again, you can get more money than you could ever handle. The first step is finding a good deal.

Chapter 6
How to find a good deal

Your Job as a real estate investor is to find a good deal.

We've been over and over it: Your job as a real estate investor is to find a good deal, and if you find a good deal there is more money than you could ever imagine available to you to fund it. So now let's talk about how to find a good deal.

I frequently tell people that I do not care if the real estate market goes up or down. I just care that it moves. I have had people telling me that I'm insane. If the market goes down that is not good. News flash: Nothing could be further from the truth. What you want as a real estate investor is volatility because it opens the way for opportunity. Volatility brings opportunity, and real estate investors are opportunity seekers. If things are fluctuating, there is opportunity, which is the lifeblood of successful real estate investment. There has never been a better time to find amazing properties and amazing deals than the market we find ourselves in right now. What you need to do is find volatility.

Thousands of people are going to experience volatile situations, and I actually want to take you through the process of volatility for a homeowner. First, something is going to happen in the life of a homeowner. They might get a zoning notice because they are illegally renting the downstairs apartment, or it may be that their roof has a problem and they can't afford to fix it, or maybe they are going through divorce or have lost a loved one and the property is going into a probate situation. It may be that they are doing a Chapter 7 or Chapter 13 bankruptcy. It may be that they have a job that is transferring them to another state and they now have two homes.

Perhaps they rented the property out and tenants have just trashed it, and now they want nothing more than to get rid of this property. Maybe they bought a property that they aren't in love with and need to move, or they need to be closer to family members. There are all kinds of volatile situations that can arise with an individual, not to mention having their interest rate go up on their loan to a level they can no longer afford. There are so many different ways that volatility relates to an individual homeowner, and that volatility becomes opportunity for you as a real estate investor. As a real estate investor it is about creating value. Money and earning money are about value exchange, when it comes down to it.

When you go into a restaurant and sit down for a nice dinner of steak and potatoes, the waiter comes out and takes your order and then goes back and tells the chef to prepare this fine meal for you. It is plated beautifully and has a fabulous aroma, and you are there with your significant other enjoying the atmosphere. When you are done with the meal, you exchange value; the value of that experience and of that steak dinner was worth more to you than the $100 you are going to pay for that dinner.

So, what you are saying is, "I am willing to exchange value. The value of the experience was worth more than the value of the money to me." Everyone has a different value proposition. For some people it would have to be enormously nice, and they will be willing to pay enormous amounts of money; and other people don't need things that nice or they are not willing to pay that much money. There is a value exchange, and understanding this value exchange will help you be successful as a real estate investor. As we talk about opportunities and we talk about people that are going through some type of a hardship or change, and the volatility in their personal lives, remember that the key to getting to those people is to offer them value. Offer them something they want that is more important than what they have. If you can trade something that you have for something they want, then you can be successful as a real estate investor. Just as importantly as your success, you can be helping people exchange what they have for what they need or want.

Next, I want to talk about volatility that happens. Once a homeowner is unable to make payments, then more volatility occurs. There is a notice of default that is filed by the financial institution hold loan, and that is basically a public notification. This notice gets recorded, and everybody can find out what is happening on that property. They are able to see who the owner is, property address, and that type of information. After that, there is a redemption period, during which the homeowner is able to try and redeem the loan before the foreclosure process begins. Once that happens; typically a notice of sales is filed, and that notice tells people who may be interested in buying this property, or that may have a lien on this property, to show up on this date, at this time, and place a bid. This is the typical process for foreclosure. The timeframes for these will vary from State to State, but this is the overall process. The redemption period is another opportunity arising for great volatility for the homeowner, who may be very receptive to any kind of offer from you. Following the redemption period, there is the auction itself, where people will show up and make bids on the property. Sometimes no bids are made.

If the highest bid that is made is for more than the lender's starting bid, then that money is due right away from the highest bidder. It is important to note that the bank's bid may or may not be for the amount that is owed on the property. It is not uncommon for banks to have bid less than what is owed because they want the property sold. In other situations the bank may go for everything that is owed, plus fees, interest, and every dollar they can tack on. It is really going to come down to the bank, the equity, the time of the money, and whatever else is going on with the bank's overall financial picture. It is also important to know whether you are bidding on the first or the second position note. There have been many disjointed bidders that found out they purchased the property subject to a first mortgage that is substantially more than the property is worth.

In the event the highest bidder is willing to pay more than the bank's bid, the highest bidder has to come with cash to pay off the lender, and the person with the winning bid then owns the property. If there are no bids, the property is now owned by the bank. If the property goes back to the bank, it typically goes to an asset manager, and there is a chance for a real estate investor to find and buy that property directly from the asset manager. If the asset manager does not end up selling that property, then he will typically list the property with an REO agent, which stands for "real estate owned." REO agents are specialists that work with banks to try and liquidate property; they are basically liquidation managers. They actually liquidate the asset. If a bank takes a property back, they have to show it on their books as real estate owned (REO), which is where that terminology came from. The problem for the banks is that the properties they own diminishes the amount of future lending they can do, and so they have to get it off their books.

Many times, banks will try to unload these properties as fast as possible. There is really nothing different between an REO Agent and a real estate agent. REO is just their specialty, meaning they specialize in helping banks liquidate properties they own in their respective areas.

In addition to REO properties, you have regular properties listed on multiple listing services. There are also HUD, FHA, and VA properties. There are short sale opportunities prior to foreclosure, and other pre-foreclosure opportunities. There are many, many, ways to find good deals, and again, your job as a real estate investor is to find a good deal. Once you find that good deal, it will attract money like a magnet, and you will be able to be successful as a real estate investor.

Chapter 7
Distressed sellers

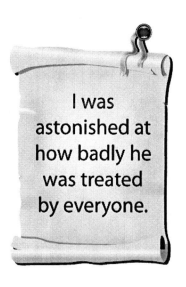

I was astonished at how badly he was treated by everyone.

We have talked all about the processes a property can go through when an owner runs into some type of hardship. Those are typically known as distressed sellers. The seller is under some type of distress, and they often have a deadline hanging over their heads. Let's spend a few minutes going over some of emotions that a distressed seller goes through.

A distressed seller is somebody that may be behind on house payments. The first thing they typically do is to bury their heads in the sand and act like nothing is wrong. A lot of them act as if they are going to win the lottery, get a new job, miraculously end up with some money from a family member, or some how it is just all going to work out. Somewhere between a month and maybe three months it sinks in, and they start to take it a little more seriously. They may get served with a legal notice, and the next thing they do is reach out for some help. They are so embarrassed that they don't necessarily tell the whole situation or they leave parts of it out. They talk to a few people, and try to find options or sometimes they will wait. Then, when they get served with the final notice and things seem out of hand, that is when they finally yell out, grasping at straws, with desperate a cry for help.

As you work with distressed sellers or people in a bad situation, you need to realize what they are going through— not only the struggle financially, but also struggle for their pride and self-esteem. It is a struggle for their whole family. Now they have to move their family from the house they have loved, and they go through so many challenges on a personal level. Understating that is key. I have had some experiences with short sales. I have actually written a book, *The*

Most Powerful Secrets to Getting Short Sales Approved, and I can tell you that these people want to be treated just like regular people. I worked with a gentleman several years ago that actually went through a short sale situation himself. When I watched him go through the short sale situation, I was astonished at how badly he was treated by everyone, including the bank. It made me want to understand the process and see what can be done, because although a financial situation may have happened in these people lives, it doesn't make them bad people. Maybe they had a business deal that went bad, a family member that got sick, or they needed to clean up their financial situation. Whether they caused it themselves or if it is a situation that they couldn't control, either way, they still want to be treated like decent human beings. They want somebody that can understand that just because they were in a bad situation financially, that doesn't mean they are worthless or failures, and it doesn't mean they can't bounce back on their feet.

As you work with distressed sellers, it is important to understand that they are just people. You need to approach them with a value exchange that will help take care of their situation and will also help make you a successful real estate investor.

Chapter 8
List Service

You need more opportunities on a day-to-day basis to find properties.

As we talk about how to find good properties, there is something that just can't be overlooked, and it might be one of the best ways to find properties; it is a list aggregator.

There are companies that provide all the information about properties that are for sale, whether they are listed with an agent, with the bank, or with a portfolio manager. They may have foreclosed properties, properties with no defaults, or a variety of other things. These are called list aggregators. We know some list aggregators, and there is the one that we feel very comfortable with that provides really good service. They are Foreclosure List Service. If you go to Do Hard Money.com and click on "find a property," you can actually sign up for a free trial, which is one of the free things we are giving away to you with this book. The free trial is going to give you seven days of unlimited access across the entire United States. So you can type in any state, any county, any city, anywhere, and you can browse through homes for sale. You can find the contact information, if that is available, for the bank, the portfolio manager, and the seller so you can jump on these opportunities.

Is a foreclosure list service going to get properties under contract for you? No. Is it going to make it easier for you to get properties under contract? Yes, because it is all about opportunity. You need more opportunities on a day-to-day basis to find properties. If you can get leads on properties that are in distressed situations, have been taken back by the bank, are currently for sale, or listed with REO agents on a daily basis, that is going to provide you with a ton of opportunity so that you can find a property and get it under contract. This list service obviously isn't free forever, but when you do pay for it, it is under $50 a month— less than a cup of coffee or a Coca Cola or Pepsi a day. You can actually get a list of all the properties that are in there with pictures. It is integrated with some other services; so you can look at everything. A foreclosure service is a great place to start finding properties, and, again, just go to DoHardMoney.com, then click on "find a property." We have arranged a free gift for you for a seven-day trial so you can play with it and see if this is something that works for you. I would encourage you to sign up for that. I think it will provide an amazing amount of value to you and will help you get some great properties under contract.

Chapter 9
Ways to approach a seller

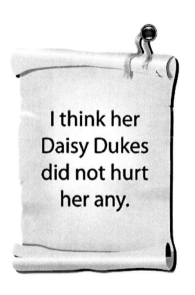

I think her
Daisy Dukes
did not hurt
her any.

You can get a list of properties and potential deals that you might be able to make offers on and eventually purchase. The next step is how you approach the sellers and what to say to them. There are books that have been written on the subject of approaching and contacting sellers. The most popular ways are through mail, through telephone, and through stop bys. I have a mentor who would find great deals by knocking on doors. He would drive through neighborhoods that he was interested in. Neighborhoods that he thought were the right price range; the neighborhood that he thought might have the right resale capability. He would look for the ugliest, most beat-up houses in those neighborhoods. Then he would stop and knock on the doors, and he'd ask them if they had any interest in selling their house. He would also knock on the doors next to the ugly beat up homes and ask the neighbors if they knew who lived next door and if they had their phone number, or if they knew anybody else that might be interested in selling their property because he was interested in buying. He had a great smile, he was personable, and he loved to talk to people, and they enjoyed talking to him. I can also tell you about a girl who would rollerblade around in neighborhoods like this, talking to people, and making her presence known. I think her short shorts or Daisy Dukes didn't hurt her any, because her assets definitely helped that, and she used them to her advantage. But she made herself known in neighborhoods. This is also known as "farming." She would knock on the doors, drop off flyers and let people know that she bought houses. She would typically buy houses that were in distress because the sellers could not sell them to anybody else. But everybody knew who she was: the chick on rollerblades with great legs. So that is the "stop by" strategy.

The other strategy you may want to use is sending mailers. Post cards are one of the most popular kinds of mailers because they are easy to see in a stack of mail. You can use small post cards and large post cards. Again, there are books written on the subject of mailing. You might find it useful to know that there are actually some computer programs that can reproduce your exact handwriting. You just hand write all of the letters of the alphabet and scan them into the program, and they can actually produce authentic-looking computer-generated handwriting. It's a lot of fun and a great way to get attention. Another technique is to actually write out your message, scan it, and then print it onto yellow paper from a legal pad. When printed directly to that yellow legal pad paper, it looks like someone really took the time to write it out. You have to be careful to line up the scan image to fit directly on the lined paper. It takes some time, but once set up you can print a lot of them. Typically, they will do half sheets that look like they are torn, and then they will put one of those on every single house they stop by. It looks like someone really personally wrote out something special just for them. So, that is another idea for stop bys, or you can even mail them out.

The other approach is to contact them by phone. Contacting by phone, I think, is going to be one of the most tempting but one of the hardest methods to use successfully. People are not generally excited to answer a phone call from somebody they do not know, and call screening happens all the time these days. A lot of people live just off cell phones rather than having home phones, and that makes them more difficult to find. There are some people that have hired private investigators to do skip traces for certain properties when they are trying to find who the owners are so they can try and make a deal happen before a property gets foreclosed on. You've got to realize there could be between $10K and $30K, or more profit; you've got to spend a little money to make a little money.

I want to talk about working with banks. You can work with asset managers, and the foreclosure list service we talked about will help you get in touch with some of these types of banks and asset managers. You can also get in touch with local banks and local credit unions. Talk to them and tell them you buy real estate. Additionally, you want to contact national managers, which you will be able to find through the foreclosure list service.

The next thing we want to talk about is working with real estate agents and how they can help you find good deals as well. We are going to devote a whole section to that coming up next. But what I want to talk to you about now is why someone will be willing to sell you their property, and the reason is simple. People will sell you their property because they can't sell it to anybody else. The majority of the time you are not going to be able to buy properties that are in great condition and move-in ready; because you can't add value to a property like that—and they can sell a cherry property to anybody. Now, occasionally you will be able to buy a property that is move-in ready if the volatility of their needs is compatible with the value you can offer them. Perhaps you can close within 5 to 10 days, and they don't have the time to spend 90 days on the market because of a job change or pending foreclosure. They may be delighted to exchange a great deal on their property for your fast money. If they can have this headache gone and never have to think about it again, they will be willing to take less money. So, "headache for money" is the value exchange. They will take less money because — they don't have to fly back and miss their family, they don't have to have a second liability, or they can go buy the new house they are ready to move into. They can't buy a new home until their present house is sold, and they might be moving across the country. They will take less money if you get the monkey off their back so they don't have to deal with it anymore.

The other thing that is important to realize is most properties are going to need work, and that is where your value comes from. If a person owns a house that is in disrepair, no one can buy it unless they are buying with cash or hard money. They can't get a bank loan on it. A new homeowner can't come in and buy the property. If the property does not have carpet, if the property has some disrepair, if it is missing a kitchen sink, if the toilet is missing, or whatever the case may be, nobody can get a loan on it. Frankly, if a property has peeling paint, they can't get a loan on that. So a lot of people look at the property. Remember, they put it with a real estate agent; they try and sell the property, and the property does not sell because it is in such disrepair that, even if somebody wanted to buy the property, they could not; that is important to realize. Even if someone wanted to buy the property, they could not because no lender is going to give them money to buy a property they cannot move into right away, and that is where "fix and flip" real estate investing comes in. You are actually taking something that is not marketable because nobody can buy it, unless they have cash. You are turning that unmarketable thing into something that has marketable value, and that is what you are getting paid for. You are getting paid for buying something and turning it into something of value.

Let's say that you made widgets. You would buy raw steel and stamp it into some type of widget, and then you would sell it to somebody. The same is true when it comes to real estate investing. You are buying a property that is raw material, just like the metal for your widgets. Then you clean the property up. You paint it. You carpet it. You do all manner of repairs and upgrades, and then you turn around and sell that property to reap the profits of your efforts. You get paid because you took on risk.

Very often banks will sell you properties as a risk transfer. If the bank has a property, they may know that they can sell it for more money, but it will probably take six months to sell. So, if the bank could get cash today, they may prefer to take less cash now and have it over with, rather than have it on their books, cramping their loaning ability and carrying the property taxes and upkeep. Sometimes the property is in good shape, and sometimes it needs work. But at the end of the day, real estate investment, from the selling bank's perspective, is a transfer of risk.

You are not taking advantage of anybody. You are actually helping people solve their problems. You are exchanging value for value. If you are not giving equally to what you are getting, they will not sell you the property. You should actually think of yourself as a real estate problem solver. You should tell people, "I solve real estate problems. If you have a real estate problem, I have the solution for you," and then you work on finding those solutions for people, customized especially for their particular problem. You are taking a problem, and you are turning it into an asset for the community, neighborhood, the seller, and for everyone else involved.

Chapter 10
Working with real estate agents

If someone
adds value it
is worth
paying for

I want to talk to you about how real estate agents can be an asset for you when it comes to investing and being a real estate investor. One commonly asked question is, "Do I have to be a real estate agent to be a real estate investor?" The answer is simply: No. I have been a licensed real estate agent for several years, and I can tell you that it comes at a price. Many times there are some legal problems or some opportunities when it comes to licensing, such as disclosures, and other kinds of issues you may run into when you are licensed. I would not recommend that you run out and get licensed. If you are already licensed, there may be some advantages. If you are not licensed, don't worry about it. When it comes to saving a few bucks here and there, one of the things you need to realize is that if someone can add value, it is worth paying for. As you work with real estate agents, you will realize that they can add a lot of value and a lot of exposure, and they can take a lot of work off your plate.

If you have a realtor carrying a share of the workload, that will free you up so you can focus on what you are best at, and then you are going to be very successful as a real estate investor. A lot of people try to improve themselves by working on their weaknesses, but I have a different philosophy. I am not going to work on my weaknesses. I am going to work on my strengths. I prefer to focus on what I am good at and let somebody else handle what I am not so good at. If you focus on your weaknesses, you are going to end up with a whole bunch of mediocre weakness; but if you focus on your strength, you could be the very best at something. So, rather than being mediocre at a lot of things that you were once weak at, why not go from being good at things to being the best at them? That is my philosophy when it comes to real estate investing, or anything that involves working with other people.

Real estate agents can be really helpful in two ways: one is buying properties, and the other is selling properties. I think it is a good idea to work with real estate agents to help find properties. Their job is to understand your criteria. They know you are buying properties under $250K in major metropolitan areas. They know you want properties that have four bedrooms and two bathrooms that are going to need some work so you can create value. Every single morning they should be looking on the multiple listing services for properties and running searches for comparables and any other information that might be helpful to your goals. Then they should come back and tell you about a good deal that fit your criteria and what it is worth, with a recommendation to buy. Some real estate agents will even go to properties for you and help estimate costs so you can just sign offers. If someone is willing to do that, then it is worth paying their commission. That adds a lot of value. Realtors are going to help you discover opportunities that you would otherwise miss. You may make $20K, $30K, or $50K on a property. It is worth paying their commissions.

The good news for buyers and agents is that you don't always have to pay. The seller of the property typically pays the buyer's agent's commission in most areas, so you may get that service practically for free. I would say, find a couple of agents that are consistent, help educate them, know what you are looking for, and let them help you find properties.

When it comes to selling properties, we do advocate working with agents.

Often times, if you work with an agent to buy the property, they will reduce the commission to sell. They are going to do a lot of things for you. First and foremost, they are going to open up the number of buyers available to you. When it comes to selling houses, it is all about the availability of buyers, and the more exposure you can get on the property, the more buyers you can get through the property. Plus, your agent can work with other agents and hold open houses, stage the home for viewing, print up stat sheets, and add other professional perks and credibility that will increase your chances of getting the property sold.

Section 2
What is a good deal?

Chapter 11
You make money when you buy

What is a
good deal
anyway?

As we have been discussing, your job is to find a good deal. You may have been asking yourself, what is a good deal, anyway? There is a common phrase that I picked up awhile ago: You make money when you buy a property; you realize your profit when you sell it. This bears repeating: You make your money when you buy; you realize your profit when you sell. The most important part of real estate investing is buying the property right, because when you sell it, the property is going to sell for whatever it is going to sell for. You have no control over what that property is going to sell for. It is going to sell for whatever a buyer is willing to pay for it. You can change the interior. You can do all kinds of repairs and updates; but, at that point, you have done everything you are going to do with that property. The only person that is going to dictate what that property is going to sell for is the next potential buyer and the marketplace. The one thing you do have control over is the price you pay to acquire it.

The lower the price you negotiate for the property, the less risk you will have in it, and the more margins for profit you are creating. It is that margin that is going to turn into money in your pocket. Consequently, it is most important to make your money when you buy a property. That is what we are going to talk about here. When you buy a property, that's when you are going to make your money.

Chapter 12
Who determines value?

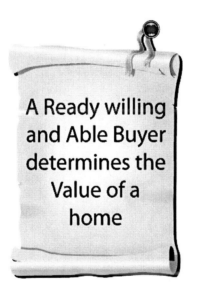

A Ready willing and Able Buyer determines the Value of a home

I have been a real estate investor and agent for over a decade. As a real estate agent, I would go on listing presentations when I first started my career. A listing presentation is when you meet with a potential seller of a home and interview with them to become their listing real estate agent. We would go out and talk with people that were interested in selling their property. We'd go into the property and we'd look around and take pictures, and then we would go back and sit down at the kitchen table. Inevitably, the question would arise, "Well Ryan, what do you think this house is worth?" and my response would be that it honestly doesn't matter what I think this house is worth; it matters what a buyer thinks this house is worth. I can tell you its worth is based on what other buyers have paid in the neighborhood and what other houses buyers can choose from in your neighborhood now. We would go through and show them identical homes that have been purchased recently or that are currently on the market for sale. We would show them the real price range for recent sales and current listings, and the seller would look up and say, "Yeah, I know, but my house is worth more than all of those. My house is just nicer." Some sellers just believe that their house is better than anything else. I believe my personal house is better than anything else out there as well, but a buyer doesn't. So, the question is: who determines value? Is the buyer determining the value, or the seller? Many sellers think they are going to determine the value of their property, and nothing could be further than the truth.

The person who is going to determine value of a property is the buyer, in the context of the current market conditions, not the seller. So, whether you think your house is worth a million dollars more than the other homes on the street or not, it's irrelevant because you have no control over what that property is really worth. The new buyer is going to make that determination, depending on what all is available. The new buyer is going to look at two things: what else can he buy for the same amount of money, and what else have sold for that same amount of money. The buyer is going to compare your property to what else he could buy and what other buyers have paid for similar properties.

Chapter 13
Actives versus Solds

Buyers don't care what a home previously sold for

Let's break it down and see if we can straighten out this messy situation. I may very well put a few people in shock, and there will probably be some controversy about what I have to say. That's okay. It is important to realize that you have to use not only sold properties but also active listings to try and determine what the property will sell for. If you talk to an appraiser, he is going to say your property value must be based upon solds. Appraisal guidelines dictate that you use sold properties as comparables to justify the value. An active home hasn't sold yet, so you have no idea what it is really worth. No one has been willing to buy it yet, and it may never sell at its listed price. Actives may be a great indication for determining a listing price to keep you competitive in the market when you are selling, but solds usually determine the baseline landscape of reality that lenders are willing to put hard money behind for the buyer.

Of course, the current market conditions can make a difference. Here is the thing you've got to understand: If your marketplace is appreciating—going up in value— looking at sold homes is going to give you a true estimation of value. However, if your marketplace is depreciating, you have to look at both actives and solds. Sold properties will most likely be higher than active properties in a falling market, because what sold last month is going to be more money than people are willing to pay this month. So, if you are using sold properties for the last month in a depreciating market place, you have already overpriced or overvalued the property compared to active homes that are for sale right now. You see, you have to look from a buyer's perspective. You need to consider what else is available. If he can buy a nicer house for the same amount of money you're asking for your property today, a potential buyer is not going to care what sold last month. You have to come up with a realistic idea of what the property is worth—*to the buyer in today's marketplace.* So, it is important to look at both active properties as well as sold properties.

Active properties are your competition, when you're selling. You have to be competitive with active properties. However, in a depreciating market, if you are looking at sold properties you want to make sure that your active properties are less money than sold properties, and you are going to want the lower price of your actives or your solds. In an appreciating market, values are going up. You are going to want to look at your actives because they are competition, but you are also going to want to look at solds. We typically recommend that you price your property to be in line with the lower of the actives or solds in the same neighborhood. You might get away with a little bit higher price if it is really in an appreciating area. In that case, you might be able to get away with pricing on the actives versus pricing on the solds.

It is important to realize that a buyer doesn't care what homes sold for previously. His appraiser may care, but he won't. All he cares about is what else he can buy for the same amount of money right now; he can't buy a home that is already sold, and looking at homes that are already sold is irrelevant. Buyers are going to look at the homes for sale in this neighborhood. They are going to look at properties that suit their needs and they are going to determine which one is the nicest for the least amount of money. That is the property they are going to make an offer on. So, yes,

you do want to look at actives—
homes that are currently for sale. *And*
you want to look at solds—homes that
have recently sold in the immediate
neighborhood. You want to price
your property according to criteria
that buyers will use to determine
value. Always remember that the
buyer, not the seller, determines the
ultimate value of a property.

Chapter 14
Determining how much you can pay for a property

AARV –
Adjusted
After Repair
Value

It is going to be very, very, important as a real estate investor to determine how much you can really pay for a property, and still make a profit. At DoHardMoney, we have come up with some really good techniques to help you determine if a property is a good deal for you. There is some terminology you need to be aware of. Let's start with "ARV." ARV is simply "After Repaired Value." After Repaired Value is basically what this home will be worth once the necessary repairs are made.

When it comes to repairs, you want to make sure you are doing work that will get you more than a dollar-for-dollar return. If you put one dollar in, you want to get two dollars out. So, if you are doing carpet or paint, for instance, you want to get two dollars out for each dollar you spend. Now, there are always some repairs that you are just going to break even on.

Maybe all the doors and the garage door need to be replaced to make the property attractive and livable. If you replace the garage door, you are going to get a dollar for dollar return. You put $2,000 in, and you are going to get $2,000 out on the sales price. Or in some cases there may be repairs that you will not get anything out of.

There may be some things you won't even get a dollar for dollar return on, but you still have to get all of the basic necessities into good shape. Replacing the driveway, for instance, doesn't add value to the property. Everyone expects the driveway not to have a big crack in it that kids might fall into; they just take that for granted. So, that is not going to increase the value of the property. Just because you spend $30,000 on repairs doesn't guarantee that you are going to add $30,000 of marketable value to that property. It is important to focus on the right things, required necessities, and spend money that will get you the return you need for a profitable deal.

The things to focus on are kitchens and bathrooms. These will get you the most bang for your investment buck. Just look at the things the ladies are going to be looking for. They all want a great kitchen. They are looking for attractive, easy-to-clean bathrooms. You have to do something to make these rooms pop and give them a bit of a "wow factor." You need your potential buyers to start imagining themselves living in this home, and feeling the excitement and pride of ownership they would have if this property were their home. If you spend money on kitchens and bathrooms, many times potential homeowners will be willing to take care of things like landscaping the backyard themselves. They are willing to settle for potential in backyards and basements, but they want the kitchen, bathrooms, and curb appeal of their dreams waiting for them when they move in.

There are many things that you can do that will boost your ARV. "As-is" value is what the property is worth the way it is right now. After Repaired Value is what the property is worth once the repairs are done. There is another valuation term that is called "AARV," which is "Adjusted After Repaired Value." The way to come up with AARV is a very simple formula. You take the After Repaired Value minus the cost of the repairs, and that equals your Adjusted After Repaired Value.

For example, if the ARV is $100,000, and the repairs on the property cost you $20,000, then you would take the $100,000 (the ARV) minus the $20,000 (the cost of the repairs). You end up with $80,000, which is the Adjusted After Repaired Value, or

AARV. You need to give yourself enough room for real estate agent fees and commissions, hard money costs, closing costs, and profit margin. We believe that 70% is the magic number. You are going to spend about 10% in agency fees, closing costs, title costs, and things like helping the buyers out by discounting the price. You are going to spend another 10% for ongoing financing and upkeep of that property for your monthly payments, gas and electric, property taxes and insurance, not to mention maintenance such as watering and cutting the grass. That leaves you with about a 10% profit margin, give or take a little, so 70% is the magic number. You need a 30% margin, once you take out the cost of repairs.

If you are buying a property with an ARV value of $100,000, and the cost of the repairs is $20,000, you have an AARV of $80,000. Then, you want to take 70% of that adjusted value, which will put purchase price at $56,000 (70% of $80K). That is going to be the most you are willing to pay for that property, so you can make money after you pay all of your bills and still leave a little margin for error in case of problems or overruns. This formula has to be your rule of thumb if you want to be a successful real estate investor.

Chapter 15
Estimated values

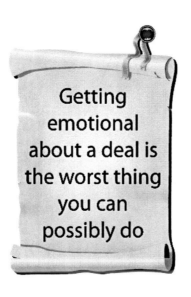

Getting emotional about a deal is the worst thing you can possibly do

We talked about active properties, or homes that are currently on the market. We talked about sold properties, which are homes that have recently sold in the neighborhood. Now I want to talk about estimating values. One of the things I've discovered is that many real estate investors get emotional about a deal, which is the worst thing you can possibly do. I was visiting with a female real estate investor. Let's call her "Sallie." Sallie purchased three properties, and she actually has all three for sale right now. Well, Sallie got emotional about all three of her properties. She bought all three properties in the same neighborhood, and they all have some little hiccups with them—one of them does not have a backyard, for example. There is actually a commercial property in the backyard, so it does not have a backyard when all the other properties in the area have backyards.

She got emotional about the deal and wanted to go in there for the thrill. Sallie did a killer fix-up, and now she is having trouble selling it. Every buyer wants a backyard. Another of her properties is right across the street from a Burger King, and you can actually smell the flame broiled hamburgers grilling as you leave for work in the morning. Everybody thinks this house is absolutely beautiful, but you can smell burgers when you wake up at 6 a.m. People just don't like the smell of burgers with their morning coffee, nor do they like people driving through with their headlights shining into their windows at night. It is really easy for a real estate investor to get emotional about a deal and overlook things. If you are working with a good hard-money lender, that lender may be your last line of defense. If he is good at his job, he is going to help you realize some problems that might not be obvious to you in your zeal to have that great house. A quality lender is not going to write a loan on it because he has no emotional attachment to the deal, which will allow him see things that you don't. A good hard-money lender is going to help you be successful.

You want an independent opinion of value when you are evaluating properties. You never want to rely on a value from a guy that is actually selling the property, because his financial incentive to keep the price as high as possible is a conflict of interest. You want to work with someone that is completely independent, as anybody with a financial incentive is not going to be acting in your best interest.

One of things that we can do for you at DoHardMoney is provide an honest estimate of the true value. For a very modest fee of less than $100 you can receive a detailed report that gives you an estimation of value. It only takes about 24 hours to run this vital report for you. This is going to give you an estimate of what the subject property is worth, and it is also going to give you a confidence score, ranging from confident, to fairly confident, to low confidence, to lack of data — four categories. The great thing is that the report is going to give you the likely value as well as an estimated value, so it is going to give you a bit of value range. The reports are going to tell you what they think the final value will be, and they are also going to give you a confidence score that is going to let you arrive at a selling price based on an unbiased opinion.

If the confidence rating in your report is lower than what you are thinking, you could still have a good deal; but if you get a report of high confidence that goes against what you are thinking, you may want to re-evaluate it. This is all done over the computer, so mistakes are possible. However, this could be a good resource to help you determine if you have a good deal or if you might be asking for trouble. Your estimated valuation report can be very helpful as a double check, but you do not need to use it as your primary determining factor.

Once you have done your comparables and anything else you might want to consider, go online to DoHardMoney.com and click on "estimated value." That will generate your report. If that report comes back in line with what you are thinking, continue with it. If that report comes back with high confidence but with a very different value, you need to do some further research. Don't cancel the deal at that point. Talk to more people in the area, meet with somebody else, call an appraiser, visit another real estate agent, pull some comparables, drive the neighborhood, do more due diligence. If you get a report with a confidence score that is not very high, but close to the value you had in mind that still doesn't mean you should cancel the deal.

I am surprised at how many people buy properties and never look at the neighborhood. If you are buying a property, you should drive the neighborhood. You should look at every home that has a "For Sale" sign, and don't just drive by. You should go inside and really check out your competition. Your competition is going to change a couple of months from now when your property is fixed up. You should be aware of whether or not the values are going down, improving, or holding steady. You should see what type of condition other active listings are in, and take pictures of them both inside and out. You should also drive by homes that have sold in the neighborhood. Those are the kinds of things you have to do if that estimated value does not come back right in line with your own estimation of its value. You should use your report of estimated value, as it can be a huge tool for your success.

Chapter 16
Property approval plus

Property Approval Plus is very inexpensive and it is going to give you critical information

We talked a little bit about comparing the estimated value from your report to the values that you get from your agent, from comparables, as well as your own valuation. If you are getting some discrepancies on the value, one of things I think you may be interested in is called "Property Approval Plus," which is actually going to give you all kinds of helpful information about the neighborhood you probably wouldn't know.

For example, it is going to list all the homes that have recently sold. It is going to give you the past history of the property, how long ago it was sold, how much it sold for, tax arrangements on property, and so forth. It is going to show you all the homes that have recently sold in the neighborhood. This will tell you if the market is depreciating or if it is appreciating. It is going to give you information about the neighborhood, how many homes are on the market, how many homes sold, and how that compares to the prior month. You can see the trends, and that information is going to be really helpful for you in determining value. This is another step. It is something you need to do. So when you are determining value, you want to start by looking at your subject property. The next thing you want to do is to look at everything in neighborhood—actives, solds, and the other homes in the neighborhood as well.

Then, once you have a rough number in mind, you want to get an estimated value for comparison. If the estimated value does not come in right, then you need to do more research. You need to talk to somebody 0else, get more comparables, drive the neighborhood again—just make sure you are not missing anything. Then the Property Approval Plus is going to tell you what is happening with the economics of the area, if homes are actually selling or not selling, if the area is depreciating, what is happening with other properties that are out in the market, what is happening with foreclosure homes in the market—all of those things and so much more. You can get it all from DoHardMoney.com. Again, it is called "Property Approval Plus." It is very inexpensive, and it is going to give you critical information that will allow you to make a better decision in determining what is a good deal.

Chapter 17
Summing it all up

You've got to have a 30% margin not including repairs

We have been talking a lot about finding a good deal. When it really comes down to it, a good deal is a property that is going to have a profitable After Repaired Value, based on active and sold comparables. You should be looking at both of those in estimating the value, knowing that you are not going to get a dollar-for-dollar return on repairs that you do to the property. Some updates and repairs are going to give you a great return for your money, and some repairs will just be an expense.

You will want to get the estimated value report to verify the accuracy of those numbers, and if your numbers are not accurate with a decent confidence score, then you need to do some more diligence, look over the neighborhood again, and talk to some other people. It is also recommended that you get a Property Approval Plus that will tell you what is happening with the marketplace, homes that have sold, what is happening to income trends, what is happening to property values—pretty much everything you need to know to determine if there is additional risk in taking on a property in that area.

At this point, once you are comfortable with all the information, you are ready to move forward and start working with a hard-money lender to get a loan approved.

When it comes to getting a good deal, as we mentioned, you've got to have a 30% margin. You've got to take the price the property will sell for, minus the cost of repairs, times 70%. In the example we looked at earlier, a house that will sell for $100,000 after doing $20,000 worth of repairs should be purchased for no more than $56,000.

How do you get all the money you can ever handle as a real estate investor? The answer is the same as the first paragraph in the book, and it bears repeating now, Find a Good Deal! I hope you have enjoyed this book, and I am certain that by following its principles you will be able to find all the money you can ever handle.

Happy Investing

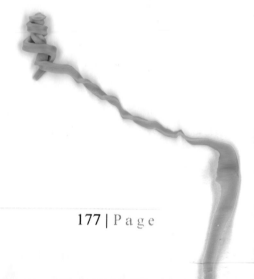

CPSIA information can be obtained at www.ICGtesting.com
Printed in the USA
BVOW020722100112

280117BV00005B/1/P

9 780982 518557